Paddling

HOENA

Paddling

HOENA

HAWAIIAN PROVERBS
AND INSPIRATIONAL QUOTES
CELEBRATING HAWAI'I'S FAVORITE PASTIME

Compiled by Tay Perry

Mutual Publishing

Library of Congress Catalog Card Number: 2006927631
ISBN-10: 1-56647-794-8
ISBN-13: 978-1-56647-794-9

First Printing, October 2006

Mutual Publishing, LLC
1215 Center Street, Suite 210 • Honolulu, Hawai'i 96816
Ph: (808) 732-1709 • Fax: (808) 734-4094
email: info@mutualpublishing.com
www.mutualpublishing.com

Printed in China

Introduction
by Tay Perry

anoe paddling has existed ever since man wanted to cross over water and discovered that a properly formed piece of wood was a more effective paddle than his hands and that a hollowed out log floated better than a solid one. Over thousands of years, canoes were crafted to become speedy seaworthy vessels. The Polynesians came to Hawai'i in voyaging canoes that were sailed with paddlers as auxiliary "engines." In recent history, events such as the monumental voyages of the *Hōkūle'a* have renewed interest in the ancient art of voyaging along with the art and science of canoe building and restoration.

In Hawai'i, outrigger canoe paddling was initially not a sport or pastime. It was a mode of travel, a means of catching fish, and a vehicle for the transport of commodities. Recreational canoe surfing, racing, and sailing were later developed to complement these more pragmatic uses of the canoe. Today, Hawaiian-style outrigger paddling is a popular sport that has spread throughout the world. Paddling is an excellent means of maintaining physical fitness, but above all, it is a lot of fun.

Paddling: Hoena, Hawaiian Proverbs and Inspirational Quotes Celebrating Hawai'i's Favorite Pastime, portrays amazing, nostalgic, and triumphant moments of men and women—Native Hawaiian and non-Hawaiian—who have experienced the exhilaration of riding the waves. Replete with vintage and contemporary images as well as words of wisdom, truth, or historical significance, this photo album about paddling celebrates this unique sport and all who continue to seek the pleasure of playing in the ocean or crossing great distances into the horizon.

Here are the canoes, get aboard
Come along and dwell in green-clad Hawai'i
A land discovered in the ocean
That rose up amidst the waves
From the very depths of Kanaloa...

– from Tommy Holmes' *The Hawaiian Canoe*

Pae mai la ka waʻa i ka ʻāina.

The canoe has come ashore.
Hunger is satisfied; or, one has arrived hither.

Today we're voyaging to learn more about our past. We're trying to recapture what has been lost in our history in the last couple hundred years. It is the hope that in better understanding our past, we're going to better understand who we are. When we understand who we are, it's going to give us a much better sense of belonging in the land that we call Hawai'i.

– Nainoa Thompson

The trick of surf riding is not learned easily
or quickly. The tourists may enjoy, however,
an equally thrilling sport in the outrigger canoe.
The beach boys take the long banana-shaped
boats, which are hollowed logs with the protecting
and balancing outrigger on the side, out to the
deep water. Favored passengers sit in the bows.
The others hang on for dear life and yell.
As the chosen wave approaches the boys holler:
"Huki! Huki!—Pull! Pull!" The canoe gains speed
under the powerful impetus of swift paddle
strokes. It lifts and starts its lunging flight...

– Don Blanding, from Glen Grant's *Hawai'i Looking Back*

He hoʻokele waʻa no ka lā ʻino.

A canoe steersman for a stormy day.

A courageous person.

"We are from the ocean, and we are water people who will end up back in the sea sooner or later."

– Solomon Aikau III, from Stuart Holmes Coleman's *Eddie Would Go*

"The canoe I perceived as lying at the heart of the old culture—it was the central object at the heart of the web of the culture. Almost everything in the culture could be related to the canoe in some way. Certainly Polynesians would not have come into existence without it."

– Herb Kane, artist and historian

Ha'alele koa wa'a i koa kanaka.

The koa canoe has departed leaving the warriors behind.

Said when a canoe goes off and leaves the people behind,
either in the water or on land.

E kaupē aku no i ka hoe a kō mai.

Put forward the paddle and draw it back.

Go on with the task that is started and finish it.

**E lauhoe mai na wa'a; i ke kā, i ka hoe;
i ka hoe, i ke kā; pae aku i ka 'āina.**

Everybody paddle the canoes together; bail and paddle,
paddle and bail, and the shore is reached.

Pitch in with a will, everybody, and the work is quickly done.

Hoʻokāhi ka ʻilau like ana.

Wield the paddles together.

Work together.

"…One man will sometimes paddle
a single canoe faster than a good boat's
crew could row a whale-boat."

– from written accounts of Europeans upon
witnessing Native Hawaiian paddlers at sea

Kihe ka ihu i ka ʻale

One who sneezes when the spray from the surf
rises at the bow of the canoe.

Said of one who braves danger with indifference.

"My father and uncle just threw me into the water from an outrigger canoe. I had to swim or else."

– Duke Kahanamoku, surfer and Olympic gold-medalist swimmer

"The building of a canoe was an affair of religion."

– Koakanu, canoe builder, from Tommy Holmes' *The Hawaiian Canoe*

'A'ohe 'auwa'a pa'a i ka hālau i ka mālie.

No canoes remain in the sheds in calm weather.

Everybody goes fishing in good weather. Also used when people turn out in great numbers to share in work or play.

He keiki kālai hoe na ka uka o Puʻukapele.

A paddle-making youth of Puʻukapele.

A complimentary expression. He who lives in the uplands,
where good trees grow, can make good paddles.
Puʻukapele is a place above Waimea Canyon on Kauaʻi.

Watch for the coral and stones of the reefs,
The waves and the billows of the ocean.
Steer the canoe over the depths of the sea.
Let the canoe travel over the waves of the sea,
Till it becomes worn, moss grown and aged.

– from Tommy Holmes' *The Hawaiian Canoe*

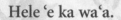

Hele ʻe ka waʻa.

The speed of a canoe.

Said of a fast traveler.

E hoʻi ka waʻa; mai hoʻopaʻa aku i ka ʻino.

Make the canoe go back;
do not insist on heading into a storm.

A plea not to do something or associate with
someone that will lead to serious trouble.

The canoe is really the central element…
to the Polynesian's survival. They're an ocean
people. Without the canoe they could not expand.
And that's why in some respects, Hawaiians today
owe their existence to the voyaging canoe.

– Nainoa Thompson

'Ōlapa ka hoe a ka lawai'a, he 'ino.

Difficult to handle is the paddle of the fisherman In a storm.

Said of one struggling against a difficult situation.
First uttered by Pele in a chant about the winds of Kaua'i.

Eia no kāhi koe e ka moamoa.

Here is the only space left, the moamoa.

Said when offering a small space or seat to a friend when every other place is occupied. As Pa'ao was leaving from Kahiki with a canoe filled to capacity, a priest, Makuakaumana, called out, asking to come along. He was offered the only available space— the sharp point at the stern of the canoe, the moamoa.

Poho pono na pe'a heke a ku ana.

A well-filled topsail helped him to arrive.

Said of a fast traveler.

My heart beats high at your venture
To buffet the raging sea!
Wild heave the waves neath the cliff-wall.
To be whelmed by Oceans might…

– from Tommy Holmes' *The Hawaiian Canoe*

'A'ohe hana a Kauhikoa; ua kau ka wa'a i ke 'aki.

Kauhikoa has nothing more to do; his canoe is resting on the block.

His work is all done.

Komo mai kau māpuna hoe.

Put in your dip of the paddle.

Pitch in.

Ku a māloʻeloʻe,
lālau na lima i ka hoe nui me ka hoe iki.

Stand up straight; reach for the big and little paddle.

Said to young people—be prepared to weather
whatever comes your way.

Pa'a 'ia iho i ka hoe uli i 'ole e īkā i ke ko'a.

Hold the steering paddle steady to keep from striking the rock.

Hold on; don't let yourself get into trouble.

Mai ka hoʻokuʻi a ka hālāwai.

From zenith to horizon.

An expression much used in prayers. In calling upon
the gods in prayers, one mentions those from the east, west,
north, south, and those from zenith to horizon.

References

Coleman, Stuart Holmes. *Eddie Would Go: The Story of Eddie Aikau, Hawaiian Hero*. Honolulu: MindRaising Press, 2001.

Evenari, Gail. *Interview with Nainoa Thompson On Wayfinding*. From Public Broadcasting Service (PBS), http://www.pbs.org/wayfinders/wayfinding3.html (accessed April 2006).

Grant, Glen, et al. *Hawai'i Looking Back: All Illustrated History of the Islands*. Honolulu: Mutual Publishing, 2000.

Hall, Sandra Kimberley. *Duke: A Great Hawaiian*. Honolulu: Bess Press, 2004.

Holmes, Tommy. *The Hawaiian Canoe*. Hanalei: Editions Limited, 1993.

Pukui, Mary Kawena. *'Ōlelo No'eau: Hawaiian Proverbs & Poetical Sayings*. Honolulu: Bishop Museum Special Publication No. 71, 1983.

Photo Credits